Weight

BLACKBIRCH PRESS

An imprint of Thomson Gale, a part of The Thomson Corporation

THOMSON

GALE

Detroit • New York • San Francisco • San Diego • New Haven, Conn. • Waterville, Maine • London • Munich

THOMSON

GALE

Consultant: Kimi Hosoume
Associate Director of GEMS (Great
    Explorations in Math and Science),
Director of PEACHES (Primary
    Explorations for Adults, Children,
    and Educators in Science),
Lawrence Hall of Science,
University of California,
Berkeley, California

For The Brown Reference Group plc
Text: Chris Woodford
Project Editor: Lesley Campbell-Wright
Designer: Lynne Ross
Picture Researcher: Susy Forbes
Illustrator: Darren Awuah
Managing Editor: Bridget Giles
Children's Publisher: Anne O'Daly
Production Director: Alastair Gourlay
Editorial Director: Lindsey Lowe

PHOTOGRAPHIC CREDITS
Alamy: Andrew Lambert 14b; **Art Explosion:** 25r; **The Brown Reference Group plc:** Edward
Allwright 1, 11t&b, Martin Norris 28; **Corbis:** Ariel Skelley 5, Tom Stewart 24; **Hemera:** 8–9,
29; **NASA:** 4; **Photolibrary.com:** Russell Burden 23, Studio 10-Scholastic 13, Lew Robertson
14t; **Photos.com:** 10, 19, 25l; **Rex:** Andy Paradise 9, SIPA 16–17, 17t, K. Arrowsmith 27;
Science & Society: 6, 7b; **Still Pictures:** Alan Watson 26; **Sylvia Cordaiy Photo Library:** 12;
Topham: 7t, 20, The Image Works/Bob Daemmrich 22, The Image Works/Joe Sohm 15.

Front cover: **The Brown Reference Group plc:** Edward Allwright

LIBRARY OF CONGRESS CATALOGING-IN-PUBLICATION DATA

Woodford, Chris.
  Weight / by Chris Woodford.
    p. cm. — (How do we measure?)
  Includes bibliographical references and index.
  ISBN 1-4103-0365-9 (lib. bdg. : alk. paper) — ISBN 1-4103-0521-X (pbk. : alk.
paper)
  1. Weights and measures. I. Title II. Series: Woodford, Chris. How do we
measure?

  QC106.W66 2005
  530.8—dc22

                                                                    2004022206

Printed and bound in Thailand
10 9 8 7 6 5 4 3 2 1

Contents

What is weight?

Have you ever tried to pick up something very heavy and not been able to? Heavy things have lots of weight. Their weight is caused by gravity. Gravity is a force that pulls things toward Earth.

Heavy things are pulled toward Earth more than light things.

Things have weight because they have mass, but mass and weight are different. Mass is the amount of matter something is made from. Matter is anything

The Moon diet

The quickest way to lose weight is to fly to the Moon! The Moon is smaller than Earth, so gravity is weaker on the Moon. Astronauts weigh around one-sixth as much on the Moon as they do on Earth.

that takes up space and has weight. Solids, such as metals, plastics, and wood, are examples of matter. Liquids, such as water, and gases, such as air, are matter, too.

A truck has more mass than a car because it contains more metal. Because a truck has more mass, gravity pulls it toward Earth more. That is why a truck weighs more than a car.

Gravity changes

Gravity is stronger or weaker at different places on Earth. Suppose a person drove a car and a truck up a mountain. At the top of the mountain, the car and the truck would weigh a little less than they do at the bottom.

They would both weigh less because gravity is weaker at the top of a mountain than at the bottom. But their mass would be the same at the top of the mountain as it was at the bottom because mass never changes.

This boy is having difficulty lifting a heavy pumpkin. The pumpkin weighs a lot because it has a lot of mass. The pumpkin has a lot of mass because it is made of a lot of matter.

History of weight

People have been weighing things for thousands of years. We know this because some people dig up places to find evidence of how others lived many years ago. They have found weights buried in 6,000-year-old graves in Egypt.

Many weights have been found from ancient Egypt. Some weights are just lumps of stone. Others are shaped like animals, including birds, beetles, and people.

Some of these old weights are simple shapes. Others are shaped like animals.

The Roman steelyard

The Romans invented a special kind of weighing machine called a steelyard. It is like a seesaw. You hang the object you want to weigh on the hooks and move the weight along the arm until the arm balances. Then the object's weight is read from a scale on the arm.

This is a Roman steelyard. It was designed to weigh things by hanging them from the hooks.

Thousands of years ago, people called the Babylonians lived in the area that is now Iraq. Like the Egyptians, the Babylonians also had weights shaped like animals.

Thousands of years ago, the ancient Romans invented the weights we now use— the ounce, pound, and ton. The Roman word for pound was *libra*. That is why the abbreviation for pound is *lb*. Around 1800, the French people became the first to use the metric system. Many other countries, but not the United States, have switched to the metric system since then.

This weight is called a Babylonian duck. People used it thousands of years ago to weigh things.

Units of weight

Most likely, you know your weight in pounds. Pounds are called imperial, English, or customary measures. A pound is a fairly small weight. An ordinary-sized bag of table sugar weighs a pound. People can measure lighter things in ounces.

There are 16 ounces in a pound. Two pencils weigh about 1 ounce.

People need bigger units to measure heavier things. Things like sacks of coal or grain are sometimes measured in hundredweights. A hundredweight is the same as 100 pounds. A big sack of flour weighs about a hundredweight.

1	1 ounce
2	2 ounces
3	4 ounces
4	8 ounces (½ pound)
5	1 pound (16 ounces)
6	2 pounds
7	3 pounds

People can measure even heavier things, like cars and trucks, using tons. A ton is sometimes called a short ton and is the same as 2,000 pounds. A small car weighs about a ton.

Pounds, hundredweight, and tons are units of weight. A unit is something that says how big a measurement is. Three pounds is a smaller weight than three hundredweight. Three hundredweight is smaller than three tons. In these examples, the number three means something different each time. The unit tells what it means.

These metal weights are used to weigh things on scales. People use a small weight to weigh something small, and a larger weight to weigh something much bigger.

How much does that weigh?

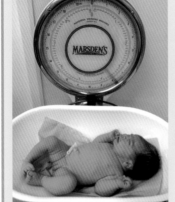

A healthy newborn baby usually weighs from around 6 to 9 pounds.

Pencil	½ ounce
Bag of table sugar	1 pound
Bag of flour	5 pounds
Baby	8 pounds
Boy (aged 8)	50 pounds
Woman	140 pounds
Man	175 pounds
Car	2 tons
Truck	10 to 50 tons

Moon
81,000,000,000,000,000,000 tons = 81 quintillion tons
Earth
600,000,000,000,000,000,000 tons = 600 quintillion tons

Metric weights

Outside the United States, many people use a set of measures called the metric system. The metric system of weights is based around the kilogram.

Kilograms
One kilogram weighs about as much as a big can of tomatoes. That is about the same as 2.2 pounds. So if a person weighs 180 pounds, we could also say that they weigh 81 kilograms (kg)—180 divided by 2.2 is 81.

There are bigger and smaller measures than pounds in the imperial system. In the same way, there are bigger and smaller weights than kilograms in the metric system.

The smallest metric weight most people use is the gram. An ounce is the same as 28 grams, so a gram is a very

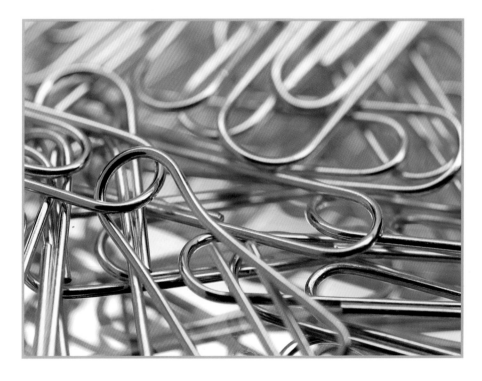

Paper clips are very light. Each one weighs only about 1 gram. There are 1,000 grams in a kilogram.

Changing weights

Imperial to metric

- 1 ounce is the same as 28 grams
  - 16 ounces, or 1 pound, is the same as 454 grams, or 0.45 kilograms
    - 1 short ton is the same as 0.9 metric tons

Metric to imperial

- 1 gram is the same as 0.04 ounces
- 1 kilogram is the same as 2.2 pounds
- 1 metric ton is the same as 1.1 short tons

small weight. A paper clip weighs about 1 gram. There are 1,000 grams in a kilogram.

Metric tons

To measure really heavy weights in the metric system, people use metric tons. A metric ton weighs 1,000 kilograms. A metric ton is slightly heavier than a short ton.

These scales show the weight in metric kilograms and imperial pounds. The pointer shows that the cereal weighs 460 grams, just over 1 pound.

Scales and balances

Children can compare their weights by sitting on a seesaw. Suppose two friends sit on either end of the seesaw at the same distance from the middle, or pivot point. When they lift up their legs, if one end of the seesaw goes down farther than the other, then the child on that end weighs the most.

Seesaws are a bit like balancing scales. If the children stop pushing the seesaw up and down, those in the air weigh less than the others.

Lots of weighing machines work like seesaws. These machines are called scales or balances. They have two pans on either side. They also have a set of weights of different sizes.

The weights can be lifted on and off the pans. To weigh an object, you put it on one pan. Then you put weights on the other pan. When the scales balance, there is the same weight on each side. If you count the weights, you know how much the object weighs.

You can also put the weights on first. To measure 10 ounces of candies, for example, a shopkeeper puts 10 ounces of weights on one pan. Then she or he pours candies into the other pan until the scales balance.

Counting by weighing

Counting coins can take a lot of time. If you go to a bank, you will see the tellers do not count coins. Instead, they weigh them. Each coin weighs the same. By weighing a bag of coins, the teller can figure out how many coins are inside.

These weighing scales have a pan either side of a central balancing point. You put the weights in one pan and the object you want to weigh in the other pan.

More ways to weigh

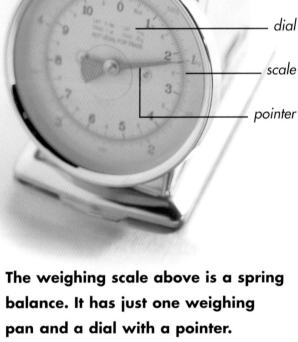

pan

dial

scale

pointer

Not all scales and balances have two pans. Some have a single pan on top and, beneath the pan, a dial with a pointer. To use a pan like this, you first set the pointer so it lines up with the zero mark. Next, you put something on the pan. The pan goes down and the pointer turns around. You then read the weight on the dial. The dial has a scale on it marked in imperial or metric units, or both.

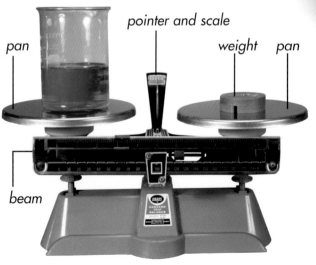

pan

pointer and scale

weight pan

beam

The weighing scale above is a spring balance. It has just one weighing pan and a dial with a pointer.

This balance (left) is different from the balance on page 13 because the pans rest on a beam. When the beam is level, the pans are of equal weight.

A truck parked atop a weighbridge. Inside the building is a special dial that shows the truck's weight.

Scales like this are sometimes called spring balances because they have a spring inside. When you put a weight on the pan, it pushes downward. That squashes the spring inside. The heavier the weight, the more the spring squashes. As the spring squashes, it moves the pointer around the dial. When the weight is taken off again, the spring goes back to its old shape.

Weighbridges

Trucks often have to be weighed if they are going onto ferries because a ship can carry only so much weight. Trucks are weighed on weighbridges. Weighbridges are like gigantic spring balances built into the road. The driver drives the truck onto the weighbridge. The truck's weight pushes the weighbridge down. A dial shows the truck's weight, just like on a spring balance.

Light weights

Light things have weight, just as heavy things do. A piece of paper does not weigh very much, but it still has weight. Even the air around us has weight. Earth's gravity pulls air toward it. That makes the cloud of gases called the atmosphere. Without the atmosphere, people could not breathe and plants could not grow. Light things do not weigh much, but sometimes people still need to weigh them.

Accurate scales

People need very accurate scales and balances to weigh very light things. They cannot use units like pounds and tons. They have to use smaller units instead.

Jewelers, for example, use a measuring system called troy weights. In the troy system, there are units of weight called ounces, pennyweights, and grains. There are 24 grains in a pennyweight. Twenty pennyweights make 1 troy ounce, and 12 troy ounces make 1 troy pound. It takes 4 troy pounds to make 1 imperial pound.

A jeweler uses a troy weight and tiny scales to measure small jewels. The troy weight is a thin slice of metal with its weight printed on it.

A scientist uses an electronic scale to measure small amounts precisely. The weight appears as numbers of milligrams on a screen.

Milligrams

In the metric system, people weigh light things using milligrams (mg). There are 1,000 milligrams in a gram, so a milligram is a very light weight. A housefly's wing weighs about 1 milligram.

Carats

A carat is a very light measurement of weight. One carat is the same as 200 milligrams, or 0.2 grams. Diamonds are usually weighed in carats. A diamond that weighs 1 carat is about ¼ inch (6 mm) in diameter.

Weight and density

Usually, bigger things weigh more than smaller ones. So, a boulder weighs more than a pebble. But that is not always true. If you have ever picked up a large gold coin, you will know that it is much heavier than it looks. So we cannot always tell how much something weighs just by looking at it.

Suppose we have a block of wood and a lump of metal of exactly the same size. Even though they are the same size, they are not the same weight. The metal weighs more than the wood because metal is more dense than wood. Density is a measure of how much matter something contains.

Invisible particles

Everything is made of matter, and all matter is made up of tiny invisible particles called atoms. The atoms that make up a piece of metal are heavier and closer together than those in wood. So a piece of metal weighs more than a piece of wood of the same size.

lead

wax

balsa wood

Blocks of lead, wax, and balsa wood of the same size weigh different amounts. Lead is the heaviest since it is the densest. Its atoms are closely packed together, so it contains the most matter. Balsa wood is the lightest since it contains the least matter. There are more spaces among its atoms.

Differing densities

Every substance on Earth has density. Density means how dense something is, or how closely its atoms are packed together. Usually solids are more dense than liquids, and liquids are more dense than gases. Gold is one of the densest solids on Earth.

Some of the least dense solids are called aerogels. They contain a huge amount of air and are sometimes called frozen smoke because they are so light.

Bars of gold like these are very heavy indeed. Gold is one of the densest solids on Earth.

Weight and floating

S ome things float on water while others do not. Wooden things are good at floating. Even huge logs will float. Metal things tend to sink. Even a paper clip will sink in water. Density is what makes one thing float and something

How low can it go?

An oil-tanker ship is a bit like an empty metal box. It takes up a certain space, or volume. When the ship is loaded with oil, it is much heavier. The volume of the ship does not change, but its mass becomes greater.

So, the more oil the tanker carries, the denser it is and the lower it floats in the water. If the tanker's density is less than the density of water, the tanker floats. If its density is more than the density of water, the tanker sinks.

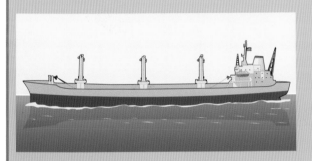

An empty oil tanker is like an empty metal box. It floats on the sea because its density is less than that of water.

When it is full of oil, the tanker floats much lower in the water because it is much denser and weighs more.

else sink. Wood is less dense than water, so wood floats. Metal is more dense than water. That is why metal sinks.

These logs float very easily on the surface of the water because they are less dense than water.

Making heavy things float

Sometimes heavy things can be made to float. A block of metal normally sinks. But if the block of metal is made into a large hollow box, it will float. That is why boats and ships float on water.

Using weights

eople need to weigh things for many reasons. One reason is so they know how much of something they are buying. Most foods are sold by weight. People pay a certain amount of money for a certain weight of food.

Weights also come in handy in cooking. Recipes tell us how to cook things. A recipe is a list of ingredients. It tells us how much of each food we have to use. Sometimes recipes

This girl is making a cake. She is using weighing scales and measuring cups to measure the ingredients.

These students are weighing things during their chemistry lesson.

ask you to measure ingredients by volume, using measurements like cups or teaspoons. At other times, people have to weigh the ingredients using scales. If we use too much or too little of something, the recipe may turn out wrong.

Weights are also important in chemistry. Chemistry is the study of materials. Many of the materials we use do not exist in nature. People have to make them by adding two or more substances together.

Chemistry is like cooking. We have to weigh chemicals before we can join them in new ways to create new chemicals.

Chemical weights

In chemistry there are more than 100 different substances called elements. Every substance on Earth is made of very tiny particles called atoms. Atoms weigh very little, and chemists have special ways to weigh them. Each element is made of a different type of atom.

For example, hydrogen is made of hydrogen atoms, and gold is made of gold atoms. Hydrogen (a gas) is the lightest element known. The heaviest element that exists in nature is a metal called uranium. Uranium atoms weigh much more than hydrogen atoms.

Body weights

Doctors weigh newborn babies regularly to see if they are growing properly. As people get older, they get bigger, taller, and heavier. People often weigh themselves by standing on scales to see how healthy they are.

If you are a certain height and age, you should weigh a certain amount. If you weigh much more than this, you may be overweight. If you weigh much

A doctor weighs a girl to check that she is healthy and growing normally.

Animal weights

How much do animals weigh compared to people?

Earthworm 5 ounces, or 140 grams
Cat   8 pounds, or 3.6 kilograms
Dog   80 pounds, or 36 kilograms
Human   160 pounds, or 72 kilograms
Panda   300 pounds, or 136 kilograms
Elephant   7 tons, or 6.3 metric tons
Blue whale 200 tons, or 180 metric tons

A panda weighs about 38 times more than a cat and twice as much as an adult human.

less, you may be underweight. Usually people are healthier if they are not overweight or underweight. If you eat well and do lots of exercise, your weight is probably just right.

Doctors can sometimes tell if people are healthy or unwell by weighing them. If people have lost a lot of weight, that might mean they are sick. If people have been sick and they start to put weight back on, it might mean that they are getting better again. So doctors find weighing people is very helpful.

Amazing weights

People cannot see gravity, so they cannot really see weight. But sometimes very heavy things, such as heavy birds, are hard to miss. The heaviest bird that flies is the mute swan. Even though it weighs 40 pounds (18 kilograms), it can still use its huge wings to get off the ground. About 1,000 years ago, there was a much heavier bird called the elephant bird that lived on the island of Madagascar, off the coast of South Africa. It weighed

Tiny leafcutter ants carrying leaves back to their nest. These ants can carry 30 times their body weight.

Monster food

It is not just animals that can grow to amazing weights. Around the world, people hold competitions to see how big they can grow fruit and vegetables. In 1990 someone grew a pumpkin that weighed 2,621 pounds, or 1,189 kilograms. In 2002 one man grew a pumpkin that weighed 337 pounds, or 153 kilograms. These monster foods look amazing, but often they do not taste very good.

1,100 pounds (500 kilograms), as much as seven men!

Some creatures can carry huge weights. An elephant can carry a quarter of its own weight on its back, around 1¾ tons, or 1.6 metric tons. A leafcutter ant can carry 30 times its own weight. But a rhinoceros beetle can carry 850 times its own weight. That is like a person carrying two trucks!

Weight, mass, and volume

You will need:

- Weighing scales
- Modeling clay
- Small solid rubber ball
- Empty shoebox
- Pile of books
- Pencil and paper

Learn how weight, mass, and volume are related but different.

1 Make the modeling clay into a round ball the same size as the rubber ball.

2 Now both balls have the same volume, but do they have the same weight? Weigh the ball of clay on the scales. Write down how much it weighs.

3 Now weigh the rubber ball. Write down the amount. Is it heavier or lighter than the clay ball?

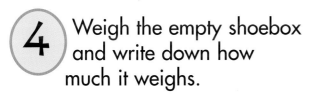

Same volume, different weights

The rubber ball and the modeling clay ball have the same volume but different weights. The shoebox has the same volume (the amount of space it takes up) as the books, but it weighs much less. The weight of an object (its heaviness or lightness) is created by the force of gravity. The more mass something has, the greater the force of gravity. Mass is the amount of matter something is made from. The shoebox is mostly empty space. So, it is made up of less matter than the books—and its mass and weight are less than that of the books.

4 Weigh the empty shoebox and write down how much it weighs.

5 Now weigh a small pile of books that match the volume of the shoebox. Write down the amount. Which object weighs the most?

Glossary

atom A tiny particle. All matter is made up of atoms.

balance A weighing device, often with two pans, used with weights.

carat A tiny weight used to weigh precious metals and gems.

density A measure of how much matter something contains.

force A push or pulling action.

gas A substance, such as air, that spreads to fill space.

gram A small unit of weight in the metric system.

gravity The force that pulls things toward Earth.

hundredweight A weight equal to 100 pounds.

imperial The common system of measurement in the United States. Pounds, ounces, inches, and feet are imperial units of measurement.

kilogram A measurement of weight in the metric system.

liquid A type of substance, such as water, that can be poured. Liquids take the shape of their container.

mass The amount of matter something contains.

matter Anything that has weight and takes up space. Solids, liquids, and gases are types of matter.

metric A system that measures things in meters and kilograms.

metric ton A large weight equal to 1,000 kilograms.

milligram A tiny weight equal to $\frac{1}{1,000}$ of a kilogram.

ounce A small weight in the imperial system.

pound A heavier weight than an ounce. There are 16 ounces in a pound.

scales A weighing device, often with one or two pans, that includes a pointer or screen showing the weight.

solid A type of substance that is neither a liquid nor a gas.

ton An imperial measurement that weighs 2,000 pounds.

troy A tiny weight used for measuring precious metals and gems.

volume The amount of space something takes up.

weighbridge A huge balance used for weighing cars and trucks.

Find out more

Books

Chris Kensler, *Secret Treasures and Magical Measures. Adventures in Measuring: Time, Temperature, Length, Weight, Volume, Angles, Shapes and Money*. Lewisville, N.C.: Kaplan, 2003.

Dorling Kindersley, *e-Science Encyclopedia.* New York: Penguin Books, 2004.

Jerry Pallotta and Rob Bolster, *Hershey's Milk Chocolate Weights and Measures*. New York: Cartwheel Books/Scholastic, 2003.

Web sites

Math Cats Balance
Try to balance objects from electrons to galaxies
www.mathcats.com/explore/ balance/balance.html

Yahooligans: Measurements and Units
A useful collection of websites about measurement
yahooligans.yahoo.com/Science_ and_Nature/Measurements_ and_Units

Your weight on other worlds
Find out how much you would weigh on Jupiter, Mars, or Saturn
www.exploratorium.edu/ ronh/weight

Index